STARFISH

Also by Pauline Uchmanowicz

Sand & Traffic
Inchworm Season

STARFISH

PAULINE UCHMANOWICZ

Poems

Twelve Winters Press

Sherman, Illinois

Text Copyright © 2016 Pauline Uchmanowicz

All rights reserved. No part of this book may be used or reproduced in any manner whatsoever without written permission except in the case of brief quotations embodied in critical articles and reviews. Contact Twelve Winters Press to inquire regarding permissions.

Starfish was first published by Twelve Winters Press in 2016.

P. O. Box 414, Sherman, Illinois 62684-0414

Visit at twelvewinters.com; email xii.winters@gmail.com; follow @twelvewinters.

Cover and interior page design by TWP Design.

Cover art copyright © 2015 Mary Ellen Strack. Used by permission. All rights reserved.

Author photos copyright © 2016 Franco Vogt. Used by permission. All rights reserved.

ISBN
978-0-9861597-7-0

Printed in the United States of America

Acknowledgments

Grateful acknowledgment is made to the editors of the following publications, where some of these poems first appeared.

Chronogram: "Stone Dogs on Brown Street," "Three Insects," "Without Company"
Commonweal: "Afterlife of a Chair," "*Geometridæ*," "Landlocked" (as "Quarry Hill Road"), "Parking Garage in January"
Crazyhorse: "In the Passing Lane," "Pinecone"
Greensboro Review: "The Motion"
Heliotrope: "Brush Burning"
Hunger Magazine: "Prophetess"
Indiana Review: "The Sore Ankle"
The Massachusetts Review: "Ideograph," "This Is Our World," "Visiting Rights"
Mudfish: "No Epithalamium" (as "Unmarried")
New American Writing: "Flowers, an Empty House and a Breakfast Roll"
Ohio Review: "Doing 'The Loop'"
Ploughshares: "*Explication de texte*"
Reading Objects 2002 and *2005* (exhibition catalogues), Samuel Dorsky Museum of Art, SUNY New Paltz: "Woodstock Sculpture," "*Fabric Merchants*"
Riverine: An Anthology of Hudson Valley Writers: "Elements of Style"
Sea Change: "Field Artillery"
A Slant of Light: Contemporary Women Writers of the Hudson Valley: "Egypt Beach, Massachusetts"
Southern Poetry Review: "the lowercase," "Mechanical Drawing"
Tinker: "Idyll"
Underwood Review: "Knee Deep in Mud My Mother," "Love and Traffic"
West Branch: "Visual Trespass"
Yet Another Small Magazine: "Tin Can Trout"

"For a Deaf Child's Sixth August" appeared in the *Chester Jones Foundation National Poetry Award Winners 1985*.

Some poems appeared in the chapbook *Inchworm Season* (Finishing Line Press).

Contents

Acknowledgments · vii

I

This Is Our World · 5
Visual Trespass · 6
The Motion · 7
Beachside Burial · 8
Afterlife of a Chair · 9
Bargain Table · 10
Elegy for a Shirt · 11
Mechanical Drawing · 12
Happiness Studies · 13
Elements of Style · 14
Prophetess · 15
No Epithalamium · 16
Tin Can Trout · 17
Without Company · 18
Swimming Hole · 20

II

For a Deaf Child's Sixth August · 23
the lowercase · 24
Egypt Beach, Massachusetts · 25
Woodstock Sculpture · 26
Tourists · 27
Knee Deep in Mud My Mother · 29
Ideograph · 30
Field Artillery · 31
Pinecone · 32
Visiting Rights · 33
Landscape Architecture · 35
Fabric Merchants · 36
Black Angel · 37
Idyll · 38
Death · 39
The Sore Ankle · 40

III

Landlocked · 45
Stone Dogs on Brown Street · 46
Flowers, an Empty House and a Breakfast Roll · 47
Dispatches from a Summer Address · 48
Postmark · 49
Explication de texte · 50
Geometridæ · 51
Three Insects · 52
Atlas of Lost Acoustics · 53
Love and Traffic · 54
Canticle · 55
Doing "The Loop" · 56
Brush Burning · 57
Parking Garage in January · 58
In the Passing Lane · 59
Writing My Mother's Obituary · 60

About the Author · 63

For Jim Spencer

STARFISH

I

This Is Our World

Scallop shells, hostages in my palms,
I look to for guidance, shoreline

receding near a mesh fence
that my body cannot pass through, though

my shadow passes through its shadow.
The moon zippers

through clouds like sperm
racing to ova,

like the red pupil in the iris of a fish,
finning up a pool of goddesses.

At sea level, life jackets dangle
ornament-style

from the limbs of a tree.
A damp voice seeps from the foam:

Look everywhere,
you will find what you need.

Visual Trespass

I cross a pond,
unobserved, spying
through binoculars
entangled figures,
boys, fist fighting.
Undeterred by high
grasses, the tallest
with advantage
could push the punier
pugilist in—into
the abyss, beyond
my glasses, where
in focus their bodies
pause, akimbo then
reunited in flailing
as uninformed as leaves
rustling a nearby bush.
Tiring, they shove
apart and run, as if
in play, not violence
after all. As if
at water's edge
each show of strength
meant only that
they are brothers.

THE MOTION

It tags the sky like moon gate or keyhole
just as I lean back in the tub,
blends through the red-gold leaves
and descends into the window sash,

a shirt tail tucking where the pane splits
two, this last gesture, then
the hot air balloon is lost to my flat skin

the way the horizontal hold finally controls
a television screen
so that even misplacing my buoyancy—

rising-hinge head lifting body—
like my sister missing two years
I do not recover where it hooks or lands.

Beachside Burial

Why finality,
                    beautiful middle child
      full of leukemia,

      against the surf line whitecaps
applauding as always,
                why we bury the young,

shovel in the dirt,
            anthills
      filling weedy cracks

            in flagstone paths,
why butterflies
      winking in a basket,

            mourners listening
for the missal's closing,
      hymn's amen,

      ferry foghorn's
            red-right-
returning

      hosanna,
            ashes to ashes,
sea to shining sea,

            why no one returns
      for what was left
behind?

Afterlife of a Chair

Never having believed in God,
what will become of your bare-bones frame,
coiled in rigor mortis
like a deformed steeple
at the peak of a garbage heap?

Previous addresses, those
games of musical chairs
or hallelujah choruses
can't save you now, nor can the sun,
holy and high over the transfer station.

Bargain Table

Dusk at a rummage sale,
the final browser, lifting up
a star-spangled colander,
uncovers an ounce of mercy in
nearly perfect condition,
previous owners having stored it
for special occasions only,
deep within darkened closets
next to piled suitcases
intended for quick escapes
that never materialized.

Roused to fuller attention,
the vendor quotes his
discounted price, then,
sensing buyer's hesitation,
inquires whether the customer
might like to acquire
a slightly soiled but
seldom paged-through
complete set of cardinal virtues.

Elegy for a Shirt

Remnant from games
of capture the flag,
softened by time
into second adolescence,
this hand-me-down's
longevity stares
out mirrors at
my middle age.

Former flannel
of my brother,
one day finally
relinquished
to a closet reliquary,
will hang beside
our deceased father's
checkered woolen,
daring me to try on its
mortality for size.

Mechanical Drawing

Once fixtures in the halls of high school,
unapproachable boys, slender like slide rules,
supplied with graphite pencils, T-squares,
compasses and protractors,
would file to classes to manufacture
perpendicular lines, plot semicircles
and measure oblique angles,
labors as enigmatic as miniature
blue-lined boxes scoring graph paper.

Degrees apart between auto shop
and trigonometry geeks,
they frequently played slide
trombone—typically boys
who ended up sloppily
startled by the brazen beauty,
instigating flings
on forbidden quadrants of playground,
sharp and pointed like
a mechanical-drawing gadget,
her rigid spread-V legs
drafting a blueprint of the world.

Happiness Studies

Singing around a campfire
you might miss happiness,
squished between envy
and sorrow. Or find it
beside you, matter-of-factly,
watching a red-tailed hawk
catch pigeons and rats,
a retriever fetching sticks
racing back and forth
from your shared park bench.
But if whistled at, happiness
bonds: with you on tiptoe
lifting curtain rods to hang
drapes, or flat-backed
positioning drip pans to change
oil, tasks completed then
together to clink steins,
toasting sand dunes and starlight.

Elements of Style

What if poets had to pick? The ocean or the stars.
A reputation in truth telling or a prize in diplomacy?

Seabed or zodiac. Water or fire. Density or infinity.
There's travel by Chinese junk with shipwreck

Or space capsule disaster. Commerce or exploration.
Marine biologist or aeronautic engineer.

Dictating rhyme, form and meter it's either
Waves as repetition or constellations as pattern,

Tide and undertow or equinox and quasar.
Cardinal points and horizons stay in joint custody

And every bard gets clarinets, trees and the rigadoon.
Also Spanish butterflies, mountains and Dutch windmills.

Prophetess

I dream of births and deaths
"Confused cathedral," mother says

"If you dream of me don't tell me"
A horse in the room (that's panic)

Newborns stampede to my sleep
Lit by a toothed moon's shine

Buildings come to me just hours
Ahead of the wrecking ball

My teenage-suicide son's
Regular telegram arrives

He's just as tormented
On the other side

I see dust flats circling stars
Where planets form—a sign painted

These stairs reserved for pilgrims
Ascending on their knees

No Epithalamium

I prefer to study stars and yet
in a living room chair I sit
and wonder what a static television
skyline can tell me about night illumination.
Since I am not called to act
to escape into that screen's city seems safe,
for in truth, my ache: it is not theatrical.
In real-life scenes I exit obligations
not of my own invention.
Hazy from the TV's low-grade din of dots
I shut my eyes to blackness and see
a family situation, satellite commitment,
and from my womb a new planet
and another, another.

Tin Can Trout

Drinking, I begin to miss you
Our empty breakfast glasses
Still around the chessboard

Only this morning you confessed
The toothbrush we shared for months
Never belonged to you

Without Company

A lone saxophone in the distance
   mono-noting "Happy Birthday"
praises life windows up, chanting
   under lights
dangling like imitation pearls
   from a giant's ears,

tuned to the hymn of its keys.
   A playing card
face down on the walk—
   how difficult not
to guess at its value, pick it up
   and give it

significance. The body crossing
   coals is
self-correcting; a young biologist
   worships its
cells in their natural cycles:
   you cannot

live unless something dies for you.
   So when
the Samurai in a movie says:
   good company is adversary
before the bloody battle, he is
   being gracious

with death, sensing worldly places
   where air,
ocean and earth are all
   the same temperature,
where people look in your hands
   and eyes

and tell you the whole story.
		Propped
open in a shop display a purple
		case shows
nothing of value—stacked boxes
		sealed down

like paper memories at the bottom
		of a pool.
Two fools wrestle with the moon
		behind a building.
In hot sun they swim up a current
		so strong

they ride the river back with it on sticks
		on their backs
and see North America in the clouds
		as if
they look down on the sky,
		wondering what's

happening where: Do people get
		happy and
stay there? Look how fast it goes,
		this time.
I have not been in relation to them
		long enough

to be anything less than amazed by
		the peonies.

Swimming Hole

This is the world we waited for made new:
A rock beside Fourth Lake, kayaks

etching pencil-line wakes
below leafy banks where half-clad

divers on boulders appear
like early Homo sapiens, paired

geese honking twice while we
tread water, still in the time

between made and unmade,
back-road shortcuts and mistletoe-

hemlock banter novel. I think:
Any moment you will lift

my fingertips to your lips,
loss and separation merging in

the brackish estuary of palm lines
joined as green eyes fix on brown.

But you resist like faces outlined
in the moon, mouths parted

starting a kiss yet forever apart.
Listen, I say. *What is happening now*:

This is your life. Hold it in your hands.
You will have no other life.

II

For a Deaf Child's Sixth August

Noon on the porch in summer the woman
—furled like pages of a magazine
after a day at the beach,
has pulled her house plant out
of its original plastic nursery container,
ready at last to transplant it
to a durable terra cotta and seen
just how pot bound it has become
with snarled roots strangling the nucleus
these last five years without her realizing,
her regret somewhat relieved in knowing
why it has not grown much.

So you see it may be merely rain, rattling
over some morning kitchen distraction,
or the kernel of doubt the woman has tossed
like a grain of sand inside her,
that makes her look up from the tan of her hands
packing down potting soil to suddenly
see how she nurtures a tangled spirit,
when your ears wrapped in corrective aids
struggle as the machinery clicks in place
and the door to your room seals you in.

THE LOWERCASE

it's visceral the way the g
of green or ground

dips below the sentence line
planting cabbage in a child

naked to the waist
seated before a bowl of borscht

purpling herself with a spoon
turned sideways

as brain gears crank
in ukrainian and english—

muse or lucky ear—
whatever her secret

may she never in any language
suffer from onomatophobia

or fear stars calling fields miracles
whether or not we name them

Egypt Beach, Massachusetts

A pre-swimmer practices
dead man's float, plays

duck-duck-goose, then
after lessons she drifts

back to the family
towels and umbrella,

where on his fingertip
her father spins a ball

as precisely as a planet
homes into syzygy,

the girl's attention poised
on the frontier that separates

matter from logic. Edging
toward the orb, head arced

with limbs stretched wide,
the child forms a five-

pointed starfish—she could
wish upon her own body

for mastery of flutter kick
and arm-over-arm crawl.

A flea pushes around a granule.
Time presses against nets.

Woodstock Sculpture

>   —Lily Ente (1905-1985), artist

Night 8 the artist named
your onyx form,

reclined like a sphinx
at the beach.

Waves fold behind
your Belgian marble spine,

its smoothness worthy
of a Pharaoh.

How would you feel
buried neck-high in sand?

Where do I press my ear
to hear your heart of darkness?

Tourists

They will feast on bean and cod,
quick-waddle crosswalks with toddlers

toward souvenir shops, or lean
mosquito-swollen arms clutching

road atlases out minivan windows.
Tomorrow, sunrays now shielded by visors

from their eyes they will aim for,
spreading beach blankets as waves, *shush*

shush rhyming at high-tide mark,
break riprap, wiping out squeals

surfacing deep from the lungs of towheads
with sand toys digging, their

Red Sox-cap wearing fathers
exchanging jibes on behalf of the team,

together sliding—*safe*—the bases
vacationer friendly, so the world expands

and shrinks. Then should gray overcast July
afternoon roll through only to dissipate

("If you don't like the weather, just
wait a minute"), electric fans

stirring humidity with sea breezes,
we year-rounders will rise from naps,

gather round grills—swordfish and wine—
to speak of the old days,

when THICKLY SETTLED signs meant
acre-lot neighborhoods, cranberry bog connecters

and farm stand pick-your-own corn.
Soon talk will turn to which barroom

ownership has changed hands,
who's living on a houseboat until August,

who made it big and who moved away
and who's back in town for another try,

until names of the dead—by overdose,
blood disease or drowning

(mercifully late or cruelly early)—again
pass among ourselves like lighted sparklers,

the sky's dippers replenishing its element,
as sand turns cool beneath our feet.

Knee Deep in Mud My Mother

Would you be so terrifying
uncoffined, dried earth caked on your calves,
disintegrating in a field among weeds
like an animal whose death
makes a place large and strange?

Or, they could wait, they could
place us in one box,
carry us someplace pleasant
we have never visited and then
waking beside you in a strange city
I would be home.

IDEOGRAPH

Edgy star, my acronical neighbor
leans from the ledge of her fifth-story roof

to fish the air with a rod and reel,
her line checked by a red chute,

a grammar school shaping her casting pool;
on a shore below

in a netted hat
another lures pet bees from combs,

the insects charmed by chugs of smoke,
stingers tempted, her hands ungloved:

as they hang in sync like casting a spell
by signaling semaphoric flags,

whiz means hook,
buzz honey, together waving.

Field Artillery

Stealthily as a foot soldier
Hillside on reconnaissance
Overlooking enemy camp

A thin blue heron
Camouflaged by grassy tillers
Strategizes a frog's capture

Refracted in the heart-shaped pond
Overlook Mountain's green trigon
Pitched like a command tent

Observing from a screened lookout
A veteran reconnoiters
His last look at the world

Pinecone

Pinecone on my fire escape, you sir,
giant rake-of-a-seed, need one day claim
to be extinct, so long as my genus keeps up
saluting uniforms enough to insure
each of your shingles cups a yarmulke of dust
over the plan of human to scrap the soul of human,
if tilted to scatter like shards from a grenade
flung from the manicured corporate hand
of an accountant who debits your future kin
to advertising expenses. Mute fruit, you all
of all that stood alone before mortar shrunk
stars, the sky stolen in shades of ambush,
if a viper shakes your spiny claws,
give thanks, thanks! for the dancing lesson!

VISITING RIGHTS

The father, inflating and releasing
        balloons
in diminishing size increments
        on Sunday,
seems to explain sex for his daughter,
        telling her

she will be less, then less, then less
        excited
by each projectile, and there is
        in the game
attraction, seduction and demise,
        ending finally

as she and her small, like herself
        small
cousin manage to burst them all, and she
        goes crying
after one he discards in a car.
        Between the kids

there is a love affair that lasts
        the length
of the leaves' turning this year
        (green straight
to brown in one week with no bleeding),
        but with Dad

love is infectious, part mystery,
        part
ingenuousness, that simple, that
        three-year-old.
What they mold, unplanned, is passed
        hand to hand,

like a plaster of Paris wedding bell,
        its casting
fondled, her cheek at Dad's bristles,
        her voice
ringing as then he whistles her back
        when she runs

unescorted for the road. Her play
        altered,
devotion faltering as her spry body
        wriggles
in his grasp, giving up, their limbs
        eloped.

Landscape Architecture

Sheltered in a domesticated woodland,
humbling one of those upscale country towns,
a roughly hewn gazebo lit by fireflies
implies a secular chapel, sanctified
not by a cross on its cedar cupola
but a directional arrow, copula
linking *wind* and *blows*, staked between mallard's
brass-winged migration and weathervane mount.

The gardener christens the structure a folly,
a shady place to watch pond water catch stars
while twilight unfolds, setting suitable for
summoning bride and groom to nuptials,
even should purplish clouds unexpectedly
engulf the firmament like a spreading bruise.

Fabric Merchants

—Utagawa Hiroshige (1797-1858), artist

Blue cranes begin
a mating dance
silk slipping from the bride's
white shoulder

and in wide streets
lining bamboo shops
bright kimonos
cries and flowers

Black Angel

—Feldevert Family Monument

A graveside place for trysts,
      there we wanted
its stark opposite:

        wingspans
steely as Brooklyn Bridge,
      lyrical as Hermes's,

    us a pair of hawks
          teaching our baby
bird to fly,

    hearts lifted
        above marble eyes
said to curse,

        underground
a buried lover's tale
    long done

while ours still fledgling,
        its objective
    correlative obscured

        like the angel's
obsidian shadow
    against night.

Statue oblivious
    to everlasting
        utterance.

IDYLL

Old and young assemble fixed in paintings.
Locked in place in a masterwork,
a grandfather forever reaches
across a picnic table to rive
a wishbone with his offspring, each figure

freezing on the brink of win or forfeit.
The boy can't cry then instantly forgive
or forsake forgiveness with age.
The elder won't ever with bitterness
carry rusted grudges to the grave.

Death

Guests perceive they have crashed this bash,
Though certainly all were invited
Despite never truly expecting to be.

Here, cocktails mixed by the host himself
One could settle into for eternity,
And his champagne is to die for.

Draped in a carpenter's apron,
Ready to hammer shut the lid of a coffin
Should need for such services arise,
He's the afterlife of the party,

Cordially greeting inevitable
Arrivals—modest or grand: *Come!*
Sit with me by this fire of small logs.
Say, why don't we be friends?

THE SORE ANKLE

Although explosive the world is not inflatable. His native people, the sore ankle is thinking, must be the most transient on earth and move at the fastest rate—always away from each other and always with some idea of permanence. Perfume. Glass. An egg roll. The sore ankle would like to feel like each of these things. Each time he moves he enters a place for the first time. Each day is irretrievable. He takes a lover and at times for him crossing the street is difficult.

*

Time concentrated like oxygen in a greenhouse. Hooks on which to hang hats in winter. The way the smell of soap makes us want to keep things inside. The way there is always something to think about, in time, slow time, without time—the way we keep things going—and all the sore ankle wants from death is to die unexpectedly, otherwise limits that go out not so much as up.

*

Cutting into the morning the sore ankle comes upon strangers at camp. Their mouths move, their timbres project, but the sore ankle does not listen to them, only sits on the opportunity of his own rebuttal. For this the strangers cut down trees and from the roots fashion a watering can and place it in the hands of the sore ankle. The sore ankle takes responsibility for the can and waters the cut down trees and the ground.

*

The watered land grows a suburb and the sore ankle erects a plastic structure on his own front lawn. It is a cross between a bus stop shelter and a giant terrarium. In it the sore ankle plants plants and flowers, hangs lights and little plaques like the one inscribed: RARE PLANTED 1967

*

Shorn, the sore ankle shrinks beside the moon of his own invention as if the day extends a gruesome hand that grows a glove finger by slender finger. His skin thickens and hardens from mis-healing and the sore ankle argues for a subject of great importance, for art, for the soul. A woman trudges through snow with a bundled babe and the sore ankle recoils, threatened, despising people for actually deserving a life.

*

Afternoon, hiking the woods, and the sore ankle comes upon a victim of strangulation. One eye open, the face twisted as if at the last second it had not wanted to die. The sore ankle cuts the body down and uncoils the noose then reties it into a ladder of rope which he drops down into the mouth of his own opinion. The sore ankle will not climb down the low ladder into the mouth of opinion. He prays for strength, for climate, for circumstances and the sore ankle ascends into bed. He is there now sleeping, all of his important papers, his income tax return, cuddled in the space his body forms like a spoon. The papers mere grains to be devoured in great gobbles or small chunks, depending upon his appetite when the sore ankle wakes up.

*

The sore ankle is being told the best sob story in years, and when the sore ankle replaces the telephone at the end of the call he feels something in common with the caller. He feels something in common with the caller, with his own house, with others who come and go, and it does not feel like anything retrievable, but it feels that things are in their place. The sore ankle feels guilty for ever having believed otherwise. Strange wonder that the psyche itself can feel retrievable, and the sore ankle feels guilty.

*

Revenge need not all make sense. It begins to rain. The sore ankle watches the weather from under a covering. If he throws himself into the river he will turn into a shovel or puff out his chest, a Samurai warrior, a real fighting fish. The rain subsides and it takes as long for the trees to finish dripping as it takes the sore ankle to let out that breath. The trees in their wetness bend into origami animals. But whether the sore ankle bends in joy or bends in sorrow is not known.

III

Landlocked

At the dead-end of the lane
a plaster Virgin tilts
into the weeds. She bestows
diagonal blessings
upon a vinyl-sided dwelling,
her half shell within earshot
of men fowl hunting,
behind the home's
foreclosure sign.

STONE DOGS ON BROWN STREET

If I lived alone in the home you guard
I would probably look out the window more
And notice the gestures of children playing on Sundays

You can't objectify reality the way you pack a suitcase

Passing my ex's porch I travel with impossibility
Two extended folding chairs cast empty
Shadows out of a cast-iron pot, staining a rag rug gray
A plastic kite hung witch-like from a clothesline
Flaps black against pale cornstalks while
Across the way an old woman walks, an iceberg holding a basket

Someone should crank a phonograph and be stunned by the blossoms

Flowers, an Empty House and a Breakfast Roll

Winging an equator along its mid-wall
this room patterns a fascination with ducks
in perpetual flight—this is how

I would like you to endure, even now,
as down the street from this neighbor's house
the empty space you've left wanders its spirit

like a busload of ballerinas. Last week
a plastic dinosaur the size of a cat
sat on a child's front porch, the best toy ever,

on the car radio Japanese jazz and the sylvan sun
glistened the cloaks of grazing cows.
Let us call time an activist.

Let it be always the day they call off politics,
the day three bodies form a straight line.
Let time be tender and sink in,

like a cluster of friends viewed through a lit
doorway, like baseball on TV, so airy
and clean. Let the fireflies out—cling

clang train. A garage band will play in a barn
while outside, unless for the sake of spring,
there is no good reason for the bonfire.

Dispatches from a Summer Address

Away from Halifax, driving
Trans-Canada Highway's
westbound lane, we fear not
how our lone car
like an anxious arrow twitches
through the wind, but that
—as advertised by traffic
signs—a moose, any moment,
might leap from the pines.

Groping as if for the bedroom
light switch in the dark,
I reach to take your hand,
picturing four hundred
kilometers into the future,
when you will place
upon a blue-chipped plate
a mute, pink grapefruit,
having harmed no one.

Postmark

The enchanted deer traveled to a town
where no one knew her name or recognized
her accent. She booked a room for the night
in a tiny B & B where a brook ran
beside the sitting room's west window,
out of which she sighted one of her former kind
drinking, head bent, on the opposite bank
beneath evergreens tinged with twilight,
while above the scenery the moon lifted,
writing postcards only it could decipher.

EXPLICATION DE TEXTE

Natives rubbing sticks spark the first line
only to canoe straight out of the stanza,
usurped by leaves cackling under a magnifying glass

followed in the next tercet by a distilled lesson
on the invention of matches: phosphorous discovered
1680; strike books manufactured 1889;

and just when you count yourself a third-through
captive, blindfolded in the pitch of typeset,
a firing squad shouldering muskets forms

a column of dropped knees, shots got off
at the heart of discourse answered by caesura,
tripping an enjambment chain

reaction further up the poem when, presaged by altar
candles casting apse shadows, campers flicker flash-
lights skyward towards the dangling Milky Way's

dying luminosity, making way for the turn, where
some disgruntled peasant tosses a matchstick into
a powder keg, the verse's fuse fizzles down and

time bomb detonates, its epiphany dynamited
to smithereens by penultimate fireworks as
a scout deciphers grand finale smoke signals.

GEOMETRIDÆ

To know this crepuscular
family of moths, commonly
occurring in vegetal regions,
even inhospitable tundra
far north, identify its green
and brown or yellowish
larvae, spottable everywhere
measuring ordinary life
by means of looping somites:
Surely the student has seen
clasped to a twig or across
an entry in her field guide
one such modest worm,
inching toward winged destiny.

Three Insects

1

When a dragonfly
lands lit green
on my white
porch overhang,
face pressed to
window screen
I hear below me
Buddhists chanting,
the planet
manifested as
desire their sole
tuning fork

2

Textured like
exotic fabric
straight from Mishima's
novel where the key
to a rendezvous
rests in a servant's palm
plump as a dragonfly,
a dragonfly
touches down
on printed pages
I read

Atlas of Lost Acoustics

Paging through this gazetteer
a musicologist locates B Flats,

that remote mountain enclave,
echoes audible there

few and far between;
tuning forks strewn like

discarded wishbones, across
an abandoned band camp's

forlorn trombone boneyard,
smelling of soil and doom.

The offbeat destination's deaf
conductor waves his baton

from the steps of a vacant
opera house, where distant

ancestors once performed
loveless tragedies. Here,

belfries are permanently
out of service and hymnals

all printed in sign language.
Kept in the library, the key

to this municipality is
fastened to the sign: *Quiet, Please.*

Love and Traffic

If a flag at half-mast meant someone loved you,
salt swilled in a drop of wine
did not resemble a pregnancy test,
a dictionary diagram of vocal cords
looked other than like a vagina
("open" on voice "closed" on whisper),
to give with condition meant less
than to take or birthrates could be ignored,

then we would love as ideally as driving 33
MPH through Manhattan and never hitting a red light,
forgetting how we move in traffic, alone yet
communal like cows grazing hillsides
ahead where a toll road ends us,
one right, one left of our pledges of allegiance.

Canticle

At the prairie's edge, wide-eyed cows,
tails swatting, wander toward us
like curious children encountering
foreign tourists and their strange
odors and tongues. Sensing a storm
drawing closer, the bovine herd
appears to be listening for God's voice.

Something has already ended.

A train whistle carries through the rain.

Doing "The Loop"

Cold all day till five,
corn born worthless in this state
where the sun breaks
but finally for only
five minutes or so,
and I'm driving when its flat,
last line of light sinks red,
right at the edge
of field piled field behind field.

I lose the wheel to the mind
to the night to distraction—
remember the future whole
rooms carved marble
the world receiving you prime,
the past remote: *middle voice* in Greek,
an earthworm tracing the same path slow.

This is where your soul belongs
flat on concrete
letting lights oval then blur,
elongate white
gates to New Zealand not visible by day.

Next noon, same loop and the moon
skywriting above a billboard sign:
I have learned to love this landscape,
and someday I'll just drive
through the gates of the Lazy 'N,'
tell the Iowa farmer
I like your land
still green in November.

Brush Burning

Cows stand in their own hoofprints.
Snow crows mimic snow angels,

crunched torsos winging eastward
toward afternoon light.

So the country woman knows
to stir downed branches,

piled in her bonfire
like fallen crosses,

until the last twig dies. Then
the sky will blacken

as if witnessing winter's
reincarnation,

its longest night quickening,
slickly as a slaughter blade.

Parking Garage in January

Beneath the highway, the parking garage
with its tarpaulin-tented spaces sinks
away from a gray weekday, into
the city's bedrock. Shopping-cart homeless
wander through it, gathered like congregants
flocked to a subterranean bazaar
or an underground revival meeting,
though lime deposits rain down upon them
like a post-testament plague, and traffic
choirs overhead tremble, horn sections
heralding their road-rage psalms, while
rush hour ushers in dusk then dark.

In the Passing Lane

The you inside of me today seems tangible.
A clapboard cottage beside a frozen pond: that is you.
My drive up the road: that is you too.
Like reading a sign, I see in the distance called past
you passing me the concept of constantly holding
friends in my mind, which reaffirms that all time
happens at once, as firmly as these pines line
the side of the road. In this moment, as a line of slow-
moving cars with headlights on in daylight
moves on the other side of the median strip,
I recollect last week, in the face of a youth
bound for Alaska, you, red-headed parrot of travel
set against gimmicks that make us hate the cold.
This is told to you in this and every other moment.

Writing My Mother's Obituary

Clicking branches
antagonized by wind
appear to argue in sign language
outside the hotel window.

Your cold-freeze cadaver
awaits transport a hundred miles
north across state borders
where months hence in residence
at the medical college
to incite gallows humor
around the dissecting table.

On the laptop I type place of origin
baseball and opera buff
then enumerate number of live births
but forgo mountains of washed
diapers folded by hand and fistfights
per day that you—only child
failed to squelch or understand.

Time wears a body bag—one size fits all.
What fades faster, the life or just after?

Pauline Uchmanowicz is the author of two poetry chapbooks and has received residency grants at the MacDowell Colony and Yaddo. A freelance writer in the Hudson Valley, her poems, essays, and reviews have appeared in *Crazyhorse, Ohio Review, Ploughshares, Provincetown Arts Journal, Radcliffe Quarterly, Woodstock Times, Z Magazine*, and elsewhere. She is associate professor of English and director of Creative Writing at SUNY New Paltz.

Photo by Franco Vogt

A Note on the Type

Starfish is set Adobe Garamond Pro. The typeface is based on the design of Claude Garamond (or Garamont), a printer in sixteenth-century Paris. He cut the typeface for the court of King Francis I, based on the handwriting of the king's librarian, Angelo Vergecio. Garamond's assistant, Robert Granjon, was instrumental in developing the italic type. Their collaboration on the serif face was early in Garamond's career. Both Garamond and Granjon went on to illustrious careers.

Adobe's digital version of Garamond was developed by Robert Slimbach and released in 1989. Adobe Garamond Pro followed in 2000.

Besides its versatility and elegance, the Garamond typeface is one of the most widely used digital styles because of its eco-friendliness: its slim design uses less ink than many other kindred typefaces.

www.ingramcontent.com/pod-product-compliance
Lightning Source LLC
Chambersburg PA
CBHW020958090426
42736CB00010B/1375